THE FIRST
THOUSAND
WORDS

A Picture Word Book

Heather Amery
Illustrated by Stephen Cartwright

Consultant: Betty Root

Sunflower Books

At home

bathroom

living room

bathtub

soap

faucet

bubbles

toothbrush

water

towel

sponge

shower

toothpaste

sink

toilet

bookcase

table

radio

4

radiator

wool

wallpaper

clock

carpet

cushion

record play

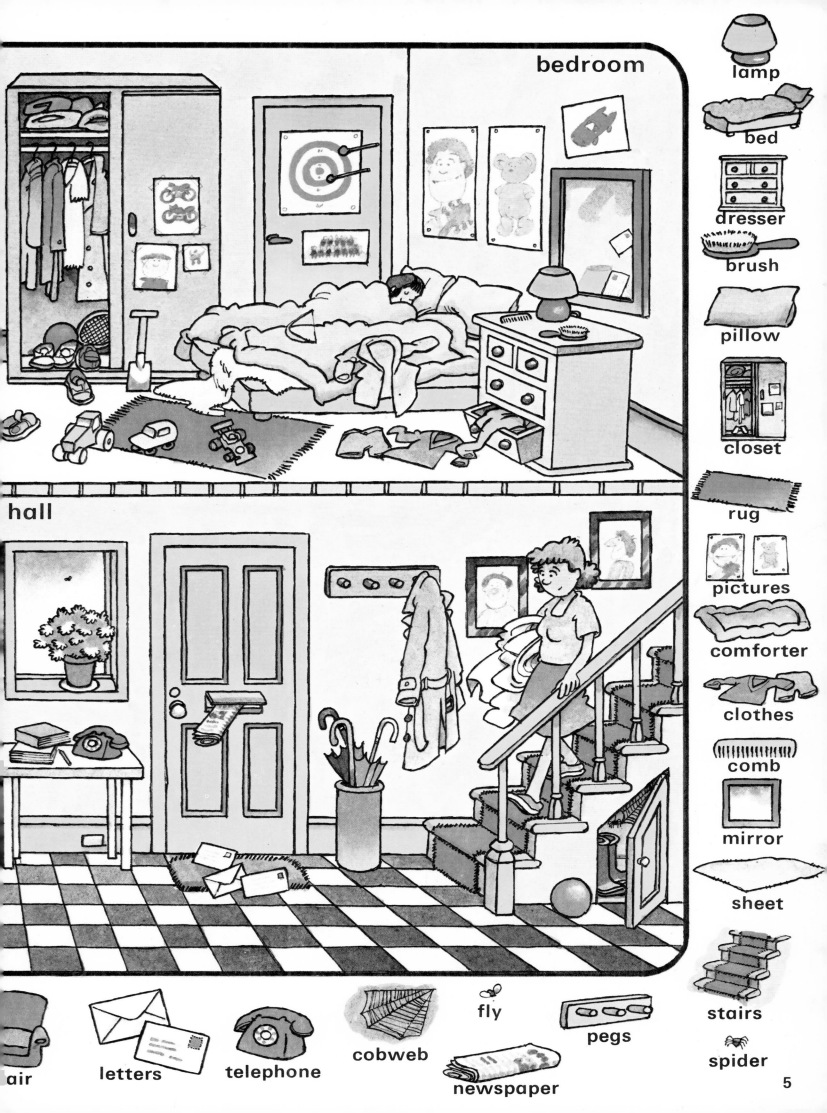

bedroom

lamp

bed

dresser

brush

pillow

closet

rug

pictures

comforter

clothes

comb

mirror

sheet

stairs

spider

hall

air

letters

telephone

cobweb

fly

newspaper

pegs

5

The kitchen

refrigerator

glasses

clock

spoons

apron

outlet

pots

saucers

iron

teakettle

mop

vacuum cleaner

sink

forks

door

dustcloth

stool

knives

polis

stove

tiles

drawer

trash

frying pan

washing
machine

dustpan

plates

ironing
board

detergent

brush

table

lightbulb

cups

teaspoons

matches

key

broom

bowls

closet 7

The yard

wheelbarrow

beehive

snail

bricks

trashcan

caterpillar

shovel

ant

pigeon

gutter

ladder

seeds

shed

8

flowers

worm

sprinkler

bone

hedge

trowel

lawn mower

path

tree

pitchfork

leaves

broom

hose

hoe

smoke

bee

rake

greenhouse

baby carriage

wasp

grass

plants

bonfire

bird's nest

sticks

9

The workshop

sandpaper

drill

bolts

tacks

saw

sawdust

hammer

file

tool box

screwdriver

board

can of paint

shavings

penknife

10

barrel

axe

nuts

tape measure

screws

ladder

nails

vise

plane

firewood

workbench

jars

wood

11

The street

gas station

ambulance

bicycle

hole

sidewalk café

sidewalk

store

traffic lights

chimney

truck

crosswalk

steps

man

12

hotel

police car

steamroller

drill

school

playground

apartment house

statue
bus
taxi
trailer
pipes
roof
market
factory
antenna
van
policeman
fire engine
house
lamp post
woman
bulldozer
church
movie theater
car
motorcycle
driver

13

The toy store

piano

cards

dolls' house

recorder

robot

harmonica

marbles

cannon

camera

beads

whistle

rocket

dice

dolls

spacemen

rocking horse

crane

steamroller

paddles

blocks

guitar

tool s

14

fishing rod

paints

clay

parachute

typewriter

boat

target

tank

soldiers

castle

bank

rain set

drums

balls

puppets

racing car

masks

trumpet

bow and arrow

gun

submarine

15

The park

ball

string

sandbox

picnic

kite

ice cream cone

dog

swings

gate

path

tadpoles

slide

16

frog

bush

roller skates

children

scoote

swans

baby

dirt

fence

stroller

birds

seesaw

flowers

puddle

ducklings

jumprope

yacht

lower bed

bench

lake

leash

duck

trees

17

The zoo

panda

bat

penguin

hippopotamus

paws

kangaroo

wing

eagle

feathers

ostrich

giraffe

wolf

monkey

pelican

gorilla

bear

beaver

lion

cubs

crocodile

18

horns

deer

camel

seal

polar bear

apes

elephant

trunk

zebra

tail

buffalo

rhinoceros

shark

goat

dolphin

leopard

whale

tiger

train tracks

guard

engine

buffers

dining car

railway cars

engineer

freight train

platform

signals

conductor

suitcases

The train station

The service station

headlights

engine

oil can

battery

oil truck

AIR

The airport

flight attendant

helicopter

runway

airplane

control tower

pilot

car wash

trunk

air pump

gas pump

wheel   wrench   tire   hood   tow truck   oil

CAR WASH   CAR WASH

21

The country

windmill

forest

cabin

rabbits

moth

fox

stream

sign post

flowers

squirrel

butterfly

birds

22 badger

hill

fox cubs

tunnel

village

owl

balloon

trailer

logs

tents

road

bridge

barge

waterfall

mountain

stones

mole

train

rocks

fisherman

canal

river

23

The farm

pond
sheep
haystack
ducks
trailer
lambs
fence
hayloft
pigsty
bull
mud
piglets
barn
stable
24 cart
farmer
pony
tractor
saddle
geese
bales of hay
sacks

truck

orchard

hen house

cowshed

cow

ducklings

cock

calf

plow

shepherd

sheep dog

turkeys

scarecrow

hens

chicks

pigs

horse

goslings

field

hay

corn

farmhouse

25

The beach

sailboat

sea

oar

lighthouse

shovel

pail

starfish

sandcastle

gull

flag

crab

sailor

sun hat

buoy

island

harbor

beach chair

motorboat

water skier

26

waves

seashell

cliff

ship

canoe

pebbles

ball

rocks

flippers

seaweed

net

paddle

fishing boat

mbrella

donkey

oil tanker

rowboat

bathing suit

rope

The school

aquarium

badge

ceiling

pencils

boys

calendar

wall

wastepaper basket

scissors

4+2 =
3-2 =

arithmetic

ruler

desk

28 photographs

paints

paper

brushes

bell

a b c d e f g
h i j k l m n o
p q r s t u v
w x y z

alphabet

boxes

books

abcdefg hijklmno pqrstuv wxyz

painting

pens

chalk

easel

floor

plants

girls

globe

glue

door handle

notebook

thumbtacks

drawing

map

crayons

lamp

blackboard

blind

eraser

teacher

29

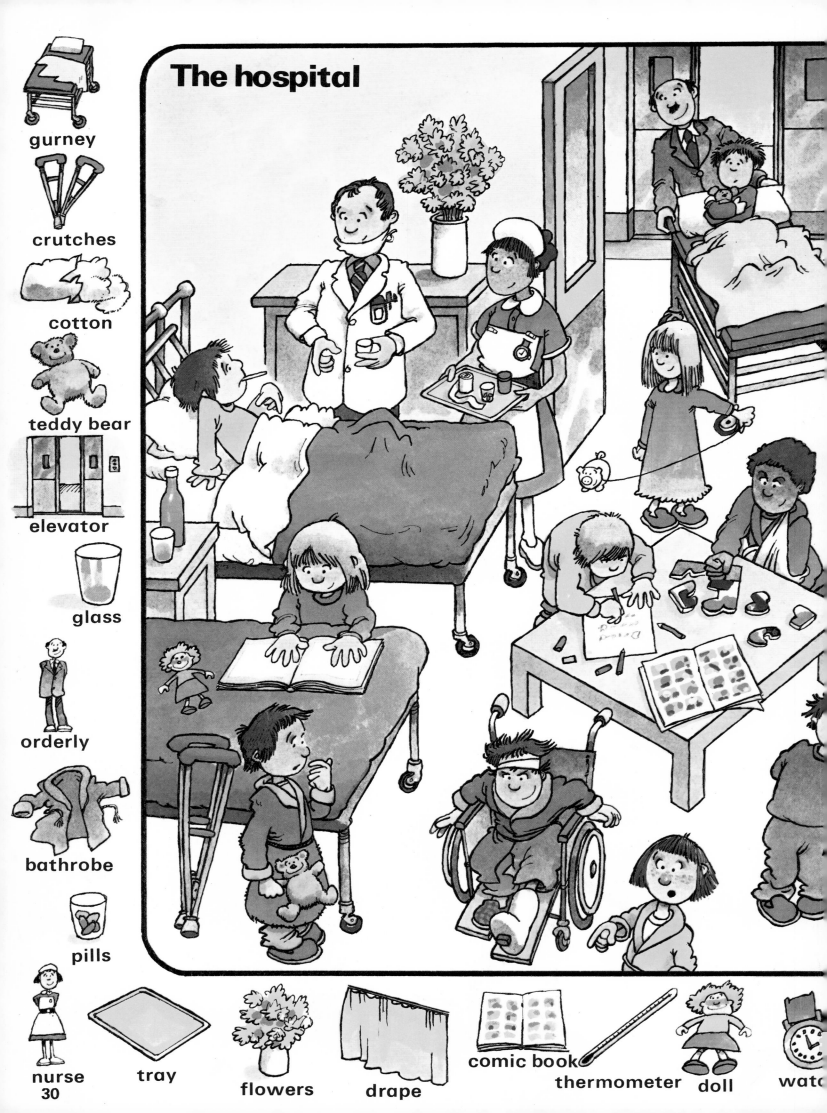

The hospital

gurney

crutches

cotton

teddy bear

elevator

glass

orderly

bathrobe

pills

nurse

tray

flowers

drape

comic book

thermometer

doll

wat

night table

medicine

slippers

pajamas

syringe

juice

nightgown

closet

television

bed

chart

cast

bandage

black eye

wheelchair

jigsaw
puzzle

doctor 31

The party

balloons

sparklers

paper hats

pudding

sandwiches

moon

candy

cookies

table cloth

records

cake

chocolate

muffins

lante

32

toys

ribbon

candles

straws

stars

packages

pudding

presents   window   jello   fireworks   paper chains   costume 33

The grocery store

bananas

grapefruit

lettuce

grapes

cauliflower

apples

carrots

leeks

pumpkin

cucumber

lemons

celery

string beans

cherries

apricots

cabbage

melon

34

CHEESE

MEA

FRUIT

FRUIT

VEGETABLES

mushrooms

tomatoes

peas

plums

raspberries

onions

peaches

pineapple

potatoes

spinach

FISH

BREAD

GROCERIES

cans

bread

butter

cheese

chicken

eggs

fish

flour

jars

meat

sausages

yogurt

basket

bottles

ssels
prouts

oranges

strawberries

bags

cash
register

scales

money

purse

shopping
cart

purse

35

Food

breakfast

lunch or dinner

coffee

chicken

jam

honey

fried eggs

milk

cream

hot chocolate

chops

beer

ham

salt

pepper

36

supper or dinner

tea

fruit juice

nuts

meat

sugar

soup

omelette

salad

stew

pancakes

rolls

rice

wine

spaghetti

catsup

37

Me

hair

eyebrow

eye

nose

cheek

mouth

lips

teeth

tongue

chin

neck

ears

head

face

shoulders

arms

elbow

hands

fingers

thumbs

back

bottom

chest

tummy

knees

legs

feet

toes

heel

My clothes

underwear

undershirt

pants

jeans

t-shirt

skirt

shirt

tie

shorts

socks

turtleneck

sweater

cardigan

tights

blouse

dress

sneakers

shoes

sandals

boots

gloves

jacket

sweatshirt

coat

handkerchief

cap

hat

belt

buttons

button holes

pockets

zipper

buckle

shoelaces

scarf

People

actor

chef

dancer

frogman

astronaut

conductor

carpenter

clown

storekeeper

soldier

policeman

farmer

singer

race car driver

mechanic

artist

40

butcher

fireman

mailman

deep-sea diver

painter

engineer

mountain climber

judge

dentist

zoo-keeper

pilot

baker

Families

father
husband

mother
wife

daughter
sister

son
brother

aunt

uncle

cousin

grandfather

grandmother

Doing things

smile

carry

bathe

think

write

crawl

build

paint

chop

break

mow

read

clean

listen

fall

wash

hide

drink

sweep

cry

laugh

dance

catch

knit

sit

42

climb

play

cook

fight

skip

pick

sleep

wait

watch

throw

talk

take

eat

sew

pull

dig

sing

win

run

jump

stand

make

buy

walk

push

43

Opposite words

good

bad

small

big

fat

thin

half

whole

cold

hot

top

soft

hard

bottom

first

last

far

few

many

near

empty

full

dirty

clean

left

high

low

44

slow

fast

easy

difficult

long

short

upstairs

downstairs

nice

nasty

over

under

front

back

wet

dry

alive

dead

dark

light

open

closed

right

old

new

out

in

Storybook words

castle

dragon

knight

giant

broomstick witch

pistol

cannon

pirate

treasur

wand

toadstool elf

dwarf

fairy

wishing well

magician

robber

desert

Indian

sheriff

cowboy

stage coac

demon

crown

page

princess

prince

sword

queen

king

palace

angel

dinosaur

prison

reindeer

sleigh

Santa Claus

wizard

ghost

bridegroom

bride

bridesmaids

monster

47

Pets

rabbits

cat

dog

goldfish

lizards

parrot

frogs

parakeets

hedgehog

silk worms

hamster

toads

puppies

pigeons

mice

snakes

kittens

turtles

48

Weather

clouds

fog

rain

frost

snow

sun

rainbow

lightning

dew

wind

mist

Seasons

spring

summer

fall

winter

Sports

boxing

cycle racing

baseball

swimming

soccer

gymnastics

high jump

skiing

auto racing

tennis

horse racing

ice skating

shooting

cricket

weight-lifting

show jumping

motorcycle racing

riding

sailing

ping pong

rowing

wrestling

basketball

judo

Colors

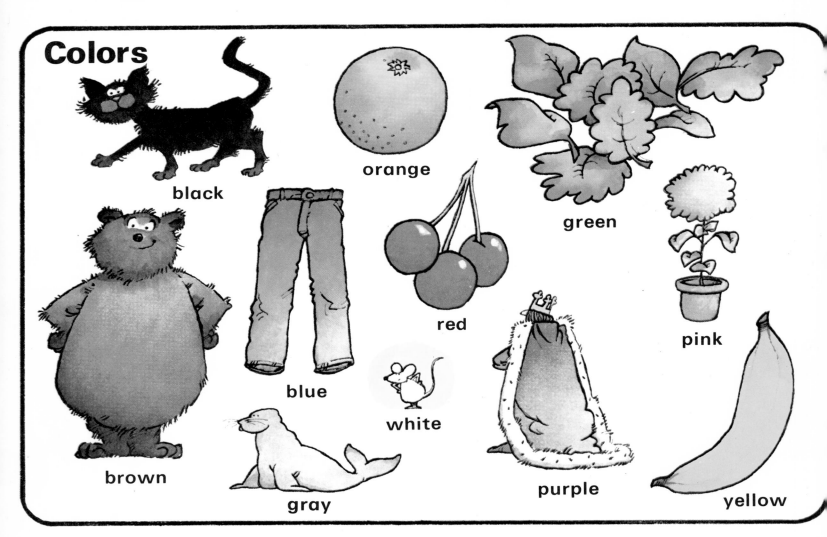

black

orange

green

red

pink

blue

white

brown

gray

purple

yellow

Shapes

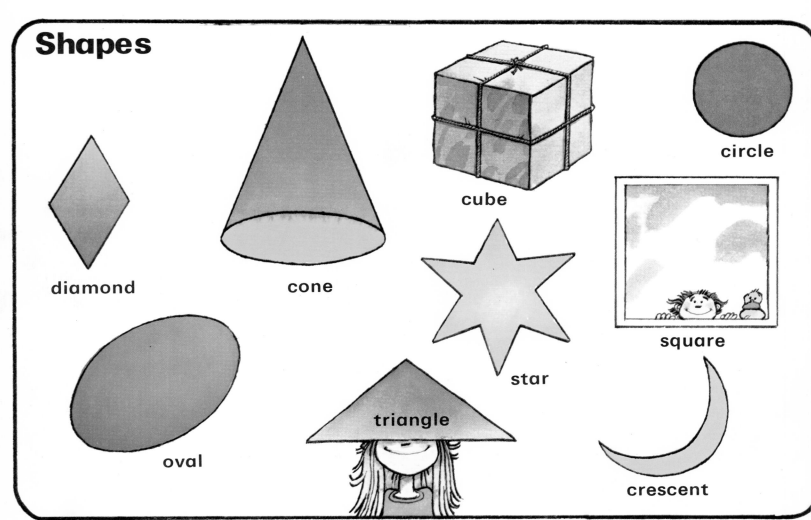

diamond

cone

cube

circle

square

star

oval

triangle

crescent

Numbers

1 one

2 two

3 three

4 four

5 five

6 six

7 seven

8 eight

9 nine

10 ten

11 eleven

12 twelve

13 thirteen

14 fourteen

15 fifteen

16 sixteen

17 seventeen

18 eighteen

19 nineteen

20 twenty

The amusement park

merry-go-round

mat

slide

Ferris wheel

bumper cars

roller coaster

ring toss

pop corn

cotton candy

fun house

rifle range

54

The circus

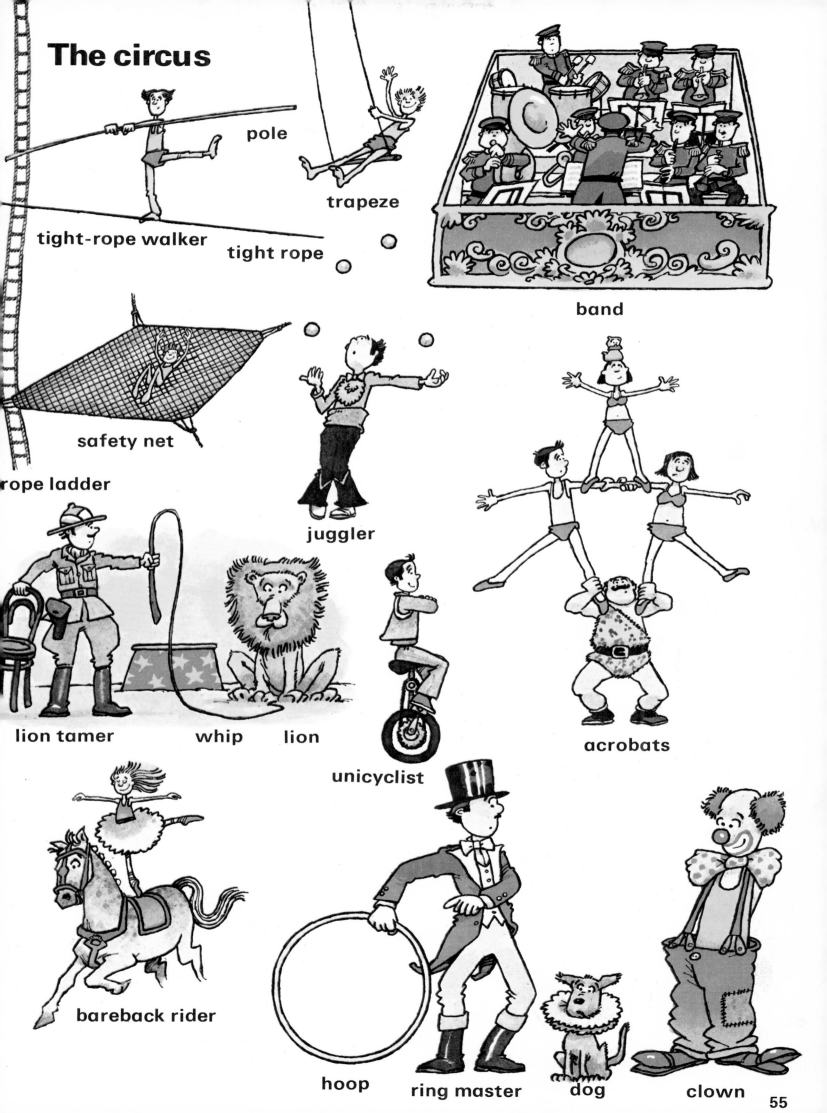

pole

trapeze

tight-rope walker

tight rope

band

safety net

rope ladder

juggler

lion tamer   whip   lion

unicyclist

acrobats

bareback rider

hoop   ring master   dog   clown

Words without pictures

Lots of words to read, say and spell

about
across
after
afternoon
again
along
all
always
am
and
another
are
as
ask
at
away

be
beautiful
because
before
behind
birthday
bought
bring
brought
burn
busy
but
by

call
came
can
chase
come
corner
could
crash

day
die
do

each
early
end
evening
every

feed
feel
fetch
find
finish
for
friend
from

game
get
give
glad
go
gone
ground
grow

happy
has
have
had
hear
heavy
help
her
here
him
his
hold
hungry
hurt

I
if
ill
is
it

jungle
just

keep
knock
know

late
leave
learn
less
let
like
line
look
lot
love
lovely

magic
meet
mend
might
month
morning
move
my
myself

name
never
next
night
no
now

of
off
once
other
our
own

pattern
please
poor
pretty
put

rich
round

sad
say
see
sell
shall
she
shine
should
show
sick
so
soon
some
sorry
speak
start
stay
stop

tell
thank
that
the
their
them
then
there
these
they
thing
thirsty
this
time
tired
to

today
tonight
tomorrow
too
try

ugly
us
use
useful

very

want
was
way
we
week
went
were
what
when
where
which
while
who
whose
why
with
work
would

year
yes
yesterday
you

Sunday
Monday
Tuesday
Wednesday
Thursday
Friday
Saturday

January
February
March
April
May
June
July
August
September
October
November
December

Words in order

This is a list of all the words in the pictures. They are in the same order as the alphabet. After each word is a number. This is the page number. On that page you will find the word and a picture.

a

acrobats, 55
actor, 40
airplane, 21
airport, 21
air pump, 21
alive, 45
alphabet, 28
ambulance, 12
animals, 18 and 19
amusement park, 54
angel, 47
ant, 8
antenna, 13
apartment house, 12
ape, 19
apple, 34
apricot, 34
apron, 6
aquarium, 28
arithmetic, 38
arrow, 15
arm, 38
artist, 40
astronaut, 40
auto racing, 50
aunt, 41
axe, 11

b

baby, 17
baby carriage, 9
back, 45
back (of body), 38
bad, 44
badge, 28
badger, 24
bag, 35
baker, 4

bales of hay, 24
ball, 16, 27
balloon, 23, 32
banana, 34
band, 55
bandage, 31
bank, 15
bareback rider, 55
barge, 23
barn, 24
barrel, 11
baseball, 50
basket, 35
basketball, 51
bat (animal), 18
bathe, 42
bathing suit, 27
bathrobe, 30
bathroom, 4
bathtub, 4
battery, 20
beads, 14
beach, 26 and 27
beach chair, 26
bear, 18
bear, polar, 19
beaver, 18
bed, 5, 31
bedroom, 5
bee, 9
beehive, 8
beer, 36
bell, 28
belt, 39
bench (park), 17
bicycle, 12
big, 44
birds, 17, 22
birds' nest, 9
black, 52
blackboard, 28
black eye, 31
blind (window), 29
blouse, 39
blow, 43
blue, 52
boat, 15
board, 10
body words, 38
bolt, 9
bone, 8
bonfire, 9
bonnet (of car), 21
book, 28
bookcase, 4
boot (for foot), 39
bottle, 35
bottom (of body), 38

bottom (drawer), 44
bow, 15
bowl, 7
boxes, 28
boxing, 50
boy, 28
bread, 35
break, 42
breakfast, 36
bricks, 8
bride, 47
bridegroom, 47
bridesmaids, 47
bridge, 23
broom, 7, 9
broomstick, 46
brother, 41
brown, 52
brush, 5, 7, 28
Brussels sprouts, 35
bubbles, 4
buckle, 39
buffalo, 19
buffers (train), 20
build, 42
bull, 24
bulldozer, 13
bumper cars, 53
buoy, 26
bus, 13
bush, 16
butcher, 41
butter, 35
butterfly, 22
button, 39
button hole, 39
buy, 43

c

cabbage, 34
cabin, 22
cake, 32
calendar, 28
calf, 25
camel, 19
camera, 14
canal, 23

candle, 33
can of paint, 10
cans, 35
candy, 32
cannon, 14, 46
canoe, 27
cap, 39
car, 13
car wash, 21
cards, 14
cardigan, 39
carpenter, 40
carpet, 4
carrot, 34
carry, 42
cart, 24
cash register, 35
cast, 31
castle, 15, 46
cat, 48
catch, 42
caterpillar, 8
catsup, 37
cauliflower, 34
ceiling, 27
celery, 34
chair, 4
chalk, 29
chart, 31
cheek, 38
cheese, 34, 35
chef, 40
cherry, 34
chest (body), 38
chick, 25
chicken, 35, 36
children, 16
chimney, 12
chin, 38
chocolate, 32
chop (wood), 42
chops (meat), 36
church, 13
circle, 52
circus, 54 and 55
clay, 15
clean, 44
clean (to), 42
cliff, 27
climb, 43
clock, 4, 6
closed, 45
closet, 5, 7, 31
clothes, 5, 39
clouds, 49
clown, 40, 55
coat, 39
cobweb, 3
cock, 25
coffee, 36
cold, 44
colors, 52

comb, 5
comforter, 5
comic book, 30
conductor (train), 20
conductor (orchestra), 40
cone, 52
control tower, 21
cook, 43
cookies, 32
corn, 25
costume, 33
cotton, 30
cotton candy, 53
country, 22 and 23
cousin, 41
cow, 25
cowboy, 46
cowshed, 25
crab, 26
crane, 14
crawl, 42
crayon, 29
cream, 36
crescent, 52
cricket (sport), 51
crocodile, 18
crosswalk, 12
crown, 46
crutches, 30
cry, 42
cub, fox, 22
cub, lion, 18
cube, 52
cucumber, 34
cup, 7
cushion, 4
cycle racing, 50

dance, 42
dancer, 40
dark, 45
daughter, 41
dead, 45
deep-sea diver, 40
deer, 19
demon, 47
dentist, 41
desert, 46
desk, 28
detergent, 7

dew, 49
diamond, 52
dice, 14
difficult, 45
dig, 43
dining car, 20
dinner, 36, 37
dinosaur, 47
dirt, 17
dirty, 44
diver, 41
doctor, 31
dog, 16, 48, 55
doing words, 42 and 43
doll, 14, 30
dolls' house, 14
dolphin, 19
donkey, 27
door, 6
door handle, 28
downstairs, 45
dragon, 46
drape, 30
drawer, 7
drawing, 29
dress, 39
dresser, 5
drill (road), 12
drill (wood), 10
drink, 42
driver, 13
drum, 15
dry, 45
duck, 17, 24
ducklings, 17
dustcloth, 6
dustpan, 7
dwarf, 46

eagle, 18
ear, 38
easel, 29
easy, 45
eat, 43
egg, 35
egg (fried), 36
eight, 53
eighteen, 53
elbow, 38
elephant, 19
elevator, 30

eleven, 53
elf, 46
engine (car), 20
engine (railway), 20
engineer, 20, 41
empty, 44
eraser, 29
eye, 38
eyebrow, 38

f

face, 38
factory, 13
fairy, 46
fall, 42
fall, 49
family, 41
far, 44
farm, 24 and 25
farmer, 24, 40
farmhouse, 25
fast, 45
fat, 44
father, 41
faucet, 4
feathers, 18
feet, 38
fence, 17, 24
Ferris wheel, 53
few, 44
field, 25
fifteen, 53
fight, 42
file, 10
finger, 38
fire, 9
fire engine, 13
fireman, 41
firewood, 10
firework, 33
first, 44
fish, 35
fisherman, 23
fishing boat, 27
fishing rod, 15
five, 53
flag, 26
flight attendant, 21
flippers, 27
floor, 29
flour, 35
flower, 8, 17, 22, 30
flowerbed, 17
fly, 5
fog, 49

food, 36 and 37
foot, 38
forest, 22
fork (table), 6
four, 53
fourteen, 53
fox, 22
fox cubs, 22
freight train, 20
fried eggs, 36
frog, 16, 48
frogman, 40
front, 45
frost, 49
fruit, 34
fruit juice, 37
frying pan, 7
full, 44
fun house, 53

g

gas pump, 21
gas station, 12, 20
gate, 16
geese, 24
ghost, 47
giant, 46
giraffe, 18
girl, 29
glass (drinking), 6, 30
globe, 29
gloves, 39
glue, 29
goat, 19
goldfish, 48
good, 44
goose, 24
gorilla, 18
gosling, 25
grandfather, 41
grandmother, 41
grape, 33
grapefruit, 34
grass, 9
gray, 52
green, 52
greenhouse, 9
groceries, 35
grocery store, 34 and 35
guard (train), 20
guitar, 14

gull, 26
gun, 15
gurney, 30
gutter, 8
gymnastics, 50

h

hair, 38
half, 44
hall, 5
ham, 36
hammer, 10
hamster, 48
hand, 38
handkerchief, 39
handle (door), 29
harbor, 26
hard, 44
harmonica, 14
hat, 39
hay, 25
hayloft, 24
haystack, 24
head, 38
headlights, 20
hedge, 8
hedgehog, 48
heel, 38
helicopter, 21
hen, 25
hen house, 25
hide, 42
high, 44
high jump, 50
hill, 22
hippopotamus, 18
hoe, 9
hole, 12
hood (car), 21
hoop, 55
home, 4 and 5
horns, 19
horse, 25
horse racing, 50
horse rider, 51
hose, 9
hospital, 30 and 31
hot, 44
hot chocolate, 36
hotel, 12
house, 13
husband, 41

i

ice cream cone, 16
ice skating, 50
in, 45
Indian, 46
iron, 6
ironing board, 7
island, 26

j

jacket, 39
jam, 36
jars, 10, 35
jeans, 39
jello, 32
jigsaw puzzle, 31
judge, 41
judo, 51
juggler, 55
juice, 31
jump, 43
jumprope, 17

k

kangaroo, 18
key, 7
      47
      d 7

59

l

ladder, 11
lake, 17
lamb, 24
lamp, 4, 29
lamp post, 13
lantern, 32
last, 44
laugh, 42
lawn mower, 9
leaf, 9
leash, 16
leaves, 9
leeks, 34
left, 44
leg, 38
lemons, 34
leopard, 19
letter, 5
lettuce, 34
light, 45
lightbulb, 6
lighthouse, 26
lightning, 49
lion, 18, 55
lion tamer, 55
lips, 38
listen, 42
living room, 4
lizards, 48
lock (canal), 23
logs, 23
long, 45
low, 44
lunch, 36

m

magician, 46
make, 43
mailman, 41
man, 12
many, 44

map, 29
marbles, 14
market, 13
mask, 15
mat, 54
matches, 7
meals, 36, 37
meat, 35, 37
mechanic, 40
medicine, 31
melon, 34
merry-go-round, 53
milk, 36
mirror, 5
mist, 49
mole, 23
money, 35
monkey, 18
monster, 47
moon, 32
mop, 6
moth, 22
mother, 41
motorboat, 26
motorcycle, 13
motorcycle racing, 51
mountain, 23
mountain climber, 41
mouth, 38
movie theater, 13
mow, 42
mud, 24
muffins, 32
mushroom, 34

n

nails, 11
nasty, 45
near, 44
neck, 38
nest, birds', 9
net, 27
new, 45
newspaper, 5
nice, 45
nightgown, 31
night table, 31
nine, 53
nineteen, 53
nose, 38
notebook, 29
numbers, 53
nurse, 30
nuts (for bolts), 11
nuts (to eat), 37